Tiananmen Square
Protests

Essential Events

TIANANMEN SQUARE
PROTESTS

BY MARCIA AMIDON LUSTED

Content Consultant
David J. Davies
Associate professor of anthropology and East Asian studies
Hamline University

ABDO
Publishing Company

CREDITS

Published by ABDO Publishing Company, 8000 West 78th Street, Edina, Minnesota 55439. Copyright © 2011 by Abdo Consulting Group, Inc. International copyrights reserved in all countries. No part of this book may be reproduced in any form without written permission from the publisher. The Essential Library™ is a trademark and logo of ABDO Publishing Company.

Printed in the United States of America,
North Mankato, Minnesota
062010
092010

Editor: Mari Kesselring
Copy Editor: Paula Lewis
Interior Design and Production: Kazuko Collins
Cover Design: Kazuko Collins

Library of Congress Cataloging-in-Publication Data
Lüsted, Marcia Amidon.
  Tiananmen Square protests / Marcia Amidon Lusted.
     p. cm. — (Essential events)
  Includes bibliographical references and index.
  ISBN 978-1-61613-686-4
  1. China—History—Tiananmen Square Incident, 1989—Juvenile literature. I. Title.
  DS779.32.L87 2010
  951.05′8—dc22

                              2010013517

TABLE OF CONTENTS

*Tank Man blocked a row of tanks traveling down
Changan Avenue in Beijing, China.*

TAKING A STAND

On June 5, 1989, a young man stepped out onto Beijing's Changan Avenue, which runs along the south side of Tiananmen Square. Carrying nothing more than a bag in each hand, he stood alone in the middle of the wide, deserted avenue. A column of Chinese tanks slowly made its way down the street toward the young man, but he did not move. As the tanks ground to a halt, the young man remained in front of them. The lead tank attempted to steer around the man, but he kept stepping into its path, forcing it to stop.

According to witnesses, the young man spoke with the soldiers inside the tank before being taken away by two other men, who may have been the Chinese secret police or just concerned bystanders. The young man's name is not known, and no one knows for sure what happened to him. But images of this young man circulated around the world, although most people in China never saw them. For the Western world, the young man's actions were a symbol of what had just occurred in Tiananmen Square.

Getting Images Out

Photographers for foreign news services in China were working before the era of digital photography. They had to resort to many methods for smuggling film and hiding it from China's police as events in Tiananmen unfolded. Charlie Cole of *Newsweek* hid one roll of Tank Man photos in a plastic bag inside a toilet tank in his hotel room. Stuart Franklin, in China for *Time* magazine, had his film smuggled out in a packet of tea by a French student who later delivered it to Franklin's company's office in Paris. Jeff Widener of the Associated Press (AP) gave his film to a college student in shorts and a T-shirt, who would not be likely to arouse suspicion. The student smuggled the film to the AP office in his underwear.

Communism

The Communist Party has dominated the Chinese government since they won the Chinese civil war in 1949. For much of the first 45 years, the government practiced a state communism similar to the Soviet Union. It owned all property and the resources needed to create products, or the "means of production." The government also closely managed all aspects of citizen's lives—even including allocating jobs and homes. The goal of this control was to reduce social inequity by giving individuals secondary importance to the collective, and to build a strong nation.

Since the early 1990s China has continued to be ruled by the Chinese Communist Party, but the party has given up the ideological commitment to communism—allowing market economics, private wealth, and individual pursuits. All collective organizations and politics, however, continue to be dominated by the party.

STUDENTS IN THE SQUARE

Tiananmen Square is located in the center of the capital city of Beijing in China. It is adjacent to the Forbidden City, the historic palace of the Chinese emperors. *Tiananmen* means "Gate of Heavenly Peace." But in early June 1989, peaceful protests at the square were about to meet a violent end.

The events that culminated in the Tiananmen Square protests and their bloody aftermath built slowly. In April and May of 1989, students began gathering peacefully in the square. They came mostly to protest the policies of their country as well as to express their desire for a new, more responsive government that allowed some of the freedoms of a democracy.

By June 3, 1989, thousands of people—mostly university students but also some intellectuals and workers—had gathered in the square.

In early April and May, students began gathering in Tiananmen Square.

Other protest groups had sprung up in other cities throughout China. The government was ready to take drastic action to dispel the protests and regain control.

That morning, the government ordered the army to clear Tiananmen Square. As darkness fell, army tanks and trucks were stationed around the perimeter of the square. Some of the protesters gathered to swear a pledge:

> *I pledge to use my young life to defend Tiananmen and to defend the republic. My head may be cut off, the blood may flow, but Tiananmen Square must not be lost. I will fight until the last person falls.* [1]

At the same time, the Chinese government broadcast a message to the people, announcing,

> *Counterrevolutionary rebellion is now taking place. [Ruffians] aim to overthrow the People's Republic of China. . . . Now we must crack down on this counterrevolutionary turmoil. . . . All citizens and students now in the square should leave immediately and let the troops carry out their tasks. We cannot guarantee the safety of those who disregard our advice.* [2]

TANK MAN

Although his image is famous around the world, the identity of the young man who became known as Tank Man is still unknown. He is believed to be a citizen of Beijing, but not a student protester. The world does not know his fate—whether he was killed or imprisoned. In many ways, Tank Man's actions demonstrate the delicate balance of power between civilians and the military during the Tiananmen Square uprisings. Though just seconds from being run over, he held his ground, and the tanks came to a halt. As with many other confrontations during that time, the military was not sure when to press forward or when to retreat in the face of adamant protesters and the civilians who tried to protect them.

For the United States and much of the Western world, the image of Tank Man came to represent the events at Tiananmen Square. At a White House news conference, President George

The Iconic Image

While the images of Tank Man have come to represent all of the events that took place around Tiananmen Square, *Newsweek* magazine photographer Charlie Cole feels that this is unfair. From his balcony at the Beijing Hotel, Cole took one of the famous pictures of the defiant man. About the image, Cole said,

In my opinion, it is regretful that this image alone has become the iconic "mother" of the Tiananmen tragedy. This tends to overshadow all the tremendous work that other photographers did up to and during the crackdown. Some journalists were killed during this coverage and almost all risked being shot at one time or another. . . . A host of others contributed to the fuller historical record of what occurred during this tragedy and we should not be lured into a simplistic, one-shot view of this amazingly complex event.[3]

H. W. Bush mentioned seeing "a single student standing in front of a tank and then . . . seeing the tank driver exercise restraint." He added, "I'm convinced that the forces of democracy are going to overcome these unfortunate events in Tiananmen Square."[4]

Democracy?

President Bush's words reveal an important disconnect between Western and Chinese views of what the Tiananmen Square protests were really about. At the time, most media outlets in the United States believed the protesters were calling for a U.S.-style democracy in China. However, this was not the case.

Democracy has different meanings within different countries and cultures. The protesters at Tiananmen wanted their country to attain the wealth and prosperity that many democratic, Western countries enjoyed during the time. They considered themselves patriotic Chinese, and some even supported the general goals of socialism. They were striving for more input in the way their country was run, more individual freedom, the ability to elect their leaders, and the removal of corrupt

government officials. But they
were not attempting to completely
overthrow the current government.

THE POWER OF TIANANMEN

The events that took place in
China in 1989, culminating in the
Tiananmen Square protests, were
more than just isolated incidents
by students who wanted change in
their government. Tiananmen was
the most recent example of patriotic
student protests that stretch back into
China's history.

While the 1989 protests failed in
that the government cracked down
on the incident and the student
movement was crushed, as a result
of the events of Tiananmen, there
have been major changes to China's
economic system. These changes
have not only affected China, but
also other parts of the world. As the
young man stood alone on Changan
Avenue in front of the advancing

Chaos

In China, there is a general fear among leaders and citizens of *luan,* or "chaos." Order is very important to the Chinese because of their history of disorder. Many people died during tumultuous periods of the country's history—such as the end of dynasties. The twentieth century had many moments of luan, most recently the Cultural Revolution. Because of this, people are fearful of luan. Many government officials viewed the protests at Tiananmen Square as the beginning of a descent into chaos. This is partly why they felt it necessary to stop the protesters.

column of Chinese tanks, he may not have known
how important his actions would be, but he believed
that his country and changes in its government were
worth fighting for. ⌐

A young girl dances during the Tiananmen Square protests on June 1, 1989.

Confucius was a Chinese philosopher.

A HISTORY OF PROTESTS

The first humans to live in China lived there more than 1 million years ago. Ancient history in China is grouped in a series of dynasties that are distinguished by the aristocratic family in power during each dynasty. This period of dynasties started around 2100 BCE and ended when China was established as a republic on January 1, 1912. Even very early Chinese civilizations commonly recorded their history in detailed accounts.

Protests, specifically student protests, have a long history in China. The first recorded student protest occurred as early as 542. About 400 years later, a crowd of approximately 30,000 students gathered again to protest corruption in the government. Many other student protests were held in the tenth and eleventh centuries.

An Educated Elite

Starting in the nineteenth century, the higher education systems in China, which only educated men, required that students pass civil service examinations to qualify for high positions in the government. The exams tested the students' knowledge of the Chinese philosopher Confucius's ideas. Confucius's teachings had been studied in China since 124 BCE. The ability to pass this exam was proof that the student was suitable to be a part of China's ruling government.

Because they had the possibility of becoming government officials, many students considered themselves part of an educated elite, and many citizens also viewed the students in this way. Students often saw it as their right and duty to have a say in their government, even before passing their exams. This led to many student-run protests.

By the mid-nineteenth century, student protests had become fairly common. Then, in 1905, China's style of education officially changed to a system more similar to that of Western countries. Education was no longer based on the study of Confucius. Instead, students in China learned about history, including history of corrupt governments. This encouraged them to challenge their own political leaders and authority figures at their schools.

Confucius

Confucius was a Chinese philosopher who was born in approximately 551 BCE. During his lifetime, China was in a state of constant change and warfare. Confucius offered his ideas on how to improve society to whomever would listen. He believed leaders should be chosen based not on their noble birth but for their moral character. In his view, an effective ruler did not just react to laws and give out punishment. Rather, he lived a moral life that served as an example to his followers.

Confucius was not well known during his lifetime, but his ideas spread after his death. The teachings of Confucius were turned into five books called the *Five Classics*. Followers of Confucius still exist today and are called Confucians. They believe that people can perfect themselves through studying both academics and virtue. Many of Confucius's sayings are still quoted around the world today.

HISTORY OF TIANANMEN SQUARE

The backdrop of the Tiananmen Square protests of 1989 was, of course, the square itself. Located in Beijing, the area that is now Tiananmen Square has long been a place for public gatherings, ceremonies, and protests—particularly those protests led by students.

The square is 1,000 acres (40 hectares) of space between the Gate of Heavenly Peace and the Front Gate. It was once a courtyard of the Forbidden City, which was constructed in the early 1400s. Only the emperor and his closest associates were allowed to enter the Forbidden City. After China became a republic in 1912, the square was opened to the public. Seven years later, the square's first highly significant protest took place.

MAY 4, 1919, PROTEST

On May 4, 1919, a student protest occurred in Tiananmen Square that would lead the way for the events of June 1989. The buildup to the May 4 protest began when journals published articles that criticized traditional Chinese culture and ineffective government by an entrenched bureaucracy. World War I had just ended, and it was a time of great change in China. China had been neutral during most of the war and, as a result, it had achieved some industrial growth during the conflict. But, in 1917, China had declared war on Germany, joining the war on the side of the Allies, and sending approximately 140,000 laborers to fight in Europe.

The students on May 4, 1919, protested to reject some aspects of the Versailles Peace Conference, which would officially end World War I. The Treaty of Versailles gave away some of China's territory, formerly colonized by Germany, to Japan. The students wanted the Chinese government to refuse to sign the treaty. They also wanted any pro-Japanese government officials ousted.

On May 4, 1919, despite warnings of government retaliation, approximately 3,000 students protested. The protest started out peacefully until a few student protesters attacked some government officials who had approved of the treaty. Police took action to end the protest and arrested 32 students. However, with this protest, the students had begun an entire movement—the May Fourth Movement.

THE MAY FOURTH MOVEMENT

Soon it was not only students who were demonstrating; others joined in as well. Laborers stopped working at Japanese-run factories, and citizens refused to buy Japanese products. This public response was mirrored 70 years later at the Tiananmen Square protests.

Some government officials believed they could increase their own power by siding with the protesters, so they took up the students' cause as well. With this help, the students obtained one of their objectives— China refused to sign the treaty with Japan. Also, students who had been arrested were freed. However, little happened to ignite change in China's bureaucracy.

The May Fourth Movement inspired many other protests throughout the twentieth century. Most of these student protests called for some form of democracy.

Female Students

After the exam-style of education was abolished in 1905, the government set up schools throughout China. However, these schools were for boys and men only. Some private schools were created for girls and women, but they were relatively few. After China became a republic in 1912, government-run schools were open to everyone. However, not everyone agreed that girls should have the same education as boys.

Part of the May Fourth Movement was about advocating for women's rights in Chinese society. More people began to believe that women should have the same educational experiences as their male counterparts. By 1922, 38 colleges and universities in China were open to women. In 1950, new laws gave women the same right to an education as men.

Many of these students felt that a democratic government would give China a stronger economy and military, which many Western democratic countries already had.

STUDENTS AND MAO ZEDONG

In 1949, the Communist Party was victorious in the Chinese civil war. Mao Zedong, the Chinese revolutionary leader, had been influenced by the May Fourth Movement and realized the importance of students and intellectuals in postwar development. He encouraged intellectuals and students to publicly offer their opinions on the government. This period of intellectual openness became known as the Hundred Flowers Campaign. It was named for a traditional slogan popular during a period in Chinese history when "a hundred flowers bloomed and a hundred schools of thought contended."[1]

But, in mid-June of 1957, all of this government criticism culminated in student protests in China's Hubei Province. The government had already decided that the criticism had gone too far and perceived the protesters as rebels attempting to overthrow the system. The government quelled the

Chairman Mao during the Cultural Revolution

protests by arresting some of the people involved and executing some student leaders.

RED GUARDS

In 1966, Mao launched the Cultural Revolution. With the Cultural Revolution, Mao hoped to create a new way of life in China. He felt that many of the country's current leaders were not revolutionary enough. With this new movement, the situation changed for students in China. Most universities were closed for the next four years. Students who supported Mao became Red Guards, a youth group movement that helped carry out changes in China put forth by the Cultural Revolution. The Red Guards targeted anyone who seemed to support a capitalist economic system. Teachers and university professors were among the earliest targets before rebels turned on party officials and local governments. The Red Guards quickly resorted to brutal tactics, beating, torturing, and sometimes even killing their perceived opponents.

The Red Guard groups soon divided into different factions. Revolutionary Red Guards, encouraged by Mao, attacked some party officials deemed pro-capitalist by forcing them from their offices and stealing and publishing secret documents. Red Guard groups began to fight against each other, causing chaotic riots and street fights. Taking note of the violence and chaos, Mao disbanded the Red Guards in 1968 and sent them to the countryside to live.

CONNECTIONS TO TIANANMEN

By the late 1980s, the students who would eventually gather in Tiananmen Square in 1989 wanted to uphold the traditions of the May Fourth Movement. They mirrored many of the practices of other early movements—including the Cultural Revolution—by their use of "big character" protest posters, seeking out factory workers to join their cause, and using bicycles for transportation. The slogans on their posters recalled famous sayings from the May Fourth Movement. In fact, many of the students felt they were continuing the protest that had begun 70 years earlier.

However, unlike earlier uprisings, the Tiananmen Square protests captured the attention of the whole world. More communication between countries was available now. Worker protests in other Communist countries had caused major changes

Student Deaths

While only one student was killed on May 4, 1919, subsequent protests often suffered greater casualties at the hands of military and government forces. For example, one student protest on May 30, 1925, resulted in the deaths of 13 students. News of these deaths outraged citizens who revered students.

in those governments. The world wondered if
the same thing could happen in China. And, the
situation in China during the 1970s and the 1980s
had set the stage for the students' plea for change.

Young Red Guards in 1967

Deng Xiaoping

SETTING THE STAGE

Just before the 1989 protests at Tiananmen Square, China had entered a new era in economics. Changes in the country's economic system greatly affected the Chinese people. The results of these changes eventually motivated students and other citizens to take action and call for change.

Deng Xiaoping took power from Mao Zedong's successor in 1977. With his revolutionary credentials and as the chairman of the Central Military, he was considered China's most powerful leader in the years after Mao's death. Deng had a new vision for China's future. He determined that the only way to make China economically and intellectually competitive was to modernize the country. He also wanted to raise the general standard of living, thereby stabilizing the country and strengthening his political control.

Deng Xiaoping

Deng Xiaoping had been a member of the Communist Party since he was a young man. But because of his enthusiasm for more liberal policies, Deng became unpopular with Mao Zedong. He was removed from office during Mao's Cultural Revolution. After Mao's death in 1976, Deng helped overthrow those who followed Mao's revolutionary policies, taking control of China.

THE FOUR MODERNIZATIONS

Deng's goal was to update four key areas: technology, agriculture, defense, and industry. Without progress in these areas, China could not hope to be globally competitive. These goals became known as the Four Modernizations. However, they could not be realized unless Deng changed how the

government managed the economy. Instead of
the government owning all profits, Deng realized the
government would need to allow for more individual
incentives to foster hard work and productivity. For
example, profits made by a single farmer were shared
with the whole community. However, if farmers were
allowed to keep some of the profits from their farms,
they would have more incentive to work harder and
take the risks needed to increase their production.
Shopkeepers and restaurant owners could operate in
a similar fashion. After Deng instituted changes that
allowed people to sell their surplus, or extra, goods
in a private market for their personal profit, many
businesses and farms grew quite quickly.

Deng also established a new "open-door" policy,
which promoted more interaction between China
and other countries. These included countries that
were former enemies, such as the United States.
Chinese government officials began visiting foreign
countries to foster economic relationships with more
technologically advanced Western countries.

China's new "open-door" policy created
links with the global market and brought in
new technology and foreign investments. Deng
encouraged other countries to build offices and

Deng Xiaoping visited the United States and met with President Jimmy Carter in 1979.

hotels in China. In 1979, Deng visited the United States, a historic event since it was the first official trip to the United States by a senior Chinese Communist official. Deng met with President Jimmy Carter in the White House to discuss China's new role.

Meanwhile, Deng instituted educational reform, which he believed was the key to speeding up technological modernization. He reintroduced the idea of an entrance exam as a way for students to enter a university, moving the education system away from politics and favoritism and back to a system based on intellect and ability.

Growing Pains

As Deng's modernizations were put into place, China's economy changed quickly in many ways. Communal land was divided up and leased to individual families in the villages. Previously neglected farms once again prospered. Some farmers became rich, particularly those who farmed close to big cities, where their surplus produced bigger profits. Business owners also began to profit.

However, this new entrepreneurial system with both private markets and government-subsidized markets also created new problems. Because food prices in private markets were now based on supply and demand, and not set by the government, farmers were able to increase the price of food. Many people working in cities and towns could no longer afford to buy it. Their wages had not increased to match the increasing cost of food. Meanwhile, the goods that were available in government-subsidized markets not operating on supply and demand steadily decreased.

Some citizens, such as the farmers, benefited from the economic changes early in the reform period, but many others did not see positive results so quickly. For many people living in cities and towns, the gap between the rich and the poor began to widen.

Intellectuals such as writers and teachers also did not experience the freedom of speech they had hoped the reforms would offer. Although they had much more freedom to express their own views when compared to the Cultural Revolution, Deng's government still closely watched them. Newspapers still printed the content that the Communist Party approved.

Intellectuals also found that Deng's interest in promoting education had its limits, especially for those not directly involved in technology or industry. Deng's main reforms centered on changing the

"Jumping into the Sea"

China's system of job allocation stayed in place until the early 1990s. Under this system, government offices assigned jobs to graduating university students. However, starting in the 1980s, students could choose to leave the state-managed system to find their own jobs. This was called *xia hai*, or "jumping into the sea" of the new market economy. If people decided to do this, however, they could not receive many government benefits.

economy and the standard of living in China rather than ideological or political changes. Professor Craig Calhoun described the Chinese economy in the period leading up to the Tiananmen Square protests:

> [The] Chinese people frequently pointed out the various shortcomings of their economy. . . . Even the most senior professors (along with engineers, doctors, and other intellectuals and professionals) made but a fraction of a taxi driver's income.[1]

Additionally, it was still common practice for college graduates to have jobs assigned to them upon graduation. Students were regularly dissatisfied with these jobs because they were often unrelated to their majors and the compensation was less than they desired.

Spreading Unrest

The discontent that some Chinese people were feeling with Deng's reforms came at a time when many other Communist governments in Eastern Europe were also beginning to experience unrest. By 1985, the Soviet Union had a new leader, Mikhail Gorbachev. He brought with him the new policies of a more democratic nature, including more freedom of information as well as free elections and speech and a reformation of the way the state was run. The idea that a Communist country could embrace liberal economic and social policies that seemed more democratic in nature began to spread beyond the Soviet Union.

Poland even ceased to be a Communist country in 1989. Czechoslovakia, East Germany, and Romania soon followed.

As these ideas spread, people living in China began to express a new criticism for the way their government was run. They began to hope that the principles of democracy and

The Solidarity Movement

The Solidarity movement in Poland greatly influenced the Tiananmen Square protests in China. Poland was a Communist country, but Solidarity was the first trade union in an Eastern European Communist country that was not controlled by the Communists. Founded in September 1980, its original leader was Lech Walesa.

Solidarity protested against its Communist government. In the early 1980s, the government attempted to destroy the union using martial law and repression tactics. However, the government was eventually forced to enter into talks with the union.

As a result of these talks, the government allowed semi-free elections in 1989. By the end of that year, a coalition government led by the Solidarity union was formed and Walesa became president in 1990. As a result of Solidarity's efforts, Poland is no longer a Communist country. Poland was one of the first of many Eastern European countries in which a people's protest movement led to a new democratic government.

the freedoms it brought—free speech, freedom of the press, freedom to choose one's own jobs, and free elections—could become part of China's modernization. Young intellectuals, students, and workers began to think that if a huge country such as the Soviet Union could begin to accept these freedoms and undergo such dramatic changes, the same could happen in their country.

A Call for More Freedom

Students and young urban workers seemed ready to lead the call for change in China. Many were becoming unemployed as the government gave up some of its control over the employment system, which resulted in fewer state-allocated jobs. Unskilled laborers found it more difficult to find work. Many intellectuals were upset over their salaries. People began to believe that something had to change in China. ⌐

Student Life

Student life at Beijing's universities in the 1980s contributed to the spread of information and ideas. Six to eight students lived in each dormitory room, with more than 9,000 students living in the 49 dormitories of Beijing University. Students spent a lot of time in their dorm rooms and interacting with their peers. As a result, they could easily disseminate radical ideas and attract fellow activists.

Students, many living in cramped dorm rooms at Beijing University, would become the main advocates for change in China.

The Democracy Wall in Beijing, China, in 1979

STUDENTS SPEAKING OUT

ollowing Deng's call for the Four
Modernizations in the late 1970s, students
and intellectuals began to speak out about the
need for a fifth modernization: democracy. They
wanted a change within Chinese society, not just

in its relationships with the rest of the world and in its technology and economy.

THE DEMOCRACY WALL

The first step in the students' protests was the Democracy Wall. The wall was located near central Beijing on a street next to a busy bus terminal. It was once simply a bulletin board, but in 1979, it quickly became the center of an entire movement. Students would meet at the wall to discuss their ideas. Later, people began hanging posters that expressed their opinions.

An electrician, Wei Jingsheng, placed an important essay on the Democracy Wall. He remembered the effect it had:

> On the night I posted my essay, "The Fifth Modernization," there were almost 300 people around the wall—even though it was in the middle of the night. . . . I

Posters

The posters hung on the Democracy Wall in Beijing were of two types. There were big character, or wall, posters, which are large posters with large handwritten Chinese characters. Posters of this kind were last used during the Cultural Revolution and are traditionally a means of protest, propaganda, and popular communication. Small character posters usually have similar content but are written on small sheets of paper in pen or pencil.

argued that democracy should be added to the government's agenda and that without it our society would never achieve the standards of living and levels of production we hoped for. After my article appeared, people began criticizing the Party more directly and confidently.[1]

Wei was one of the most influential protesters of what became known as the Democracy Wall movement. As a result of his essay, he was arrested and spent 18 years in jail.

However, students continued to speak out and publish underground magazines that were critical of the government. Students also gathered in public places, such as parks, to sing, play music, and dance, as well as talk about the need for greater freedom.

DENG SPEAKS OUT

In response to the growing Democracy Wall movement that

Wei Jingsheng

Prior to posting his essay on the Democracy Wall in Beijing, Wei Jingsheng had been a Red Guard during the Cultural Revolution. Wei wanted China to become a true democracy. Unlike many others who posted government criticism on the Democracy Wall, Wei included his real name and address.

Wei was imprisoned for a total of 18 years. At times he was on death row, and he spent five years in solitary confinement. In 1997, Wei was released from jail and exiled to the United States, where he continues to advocate for human rights and democracy in China.

had now spread to other cities in China, Deng gave a speech in March 1979 that warned against the movement and claimed two forces were at work in the protest—innocent students and counterrevolutionaries:

> *In Shanghai there is a so-called Democracy Forum. Some of its members have . . . put up big counter-revolutionary posters. . . . They allege that . . . instead of carrying out the four modernizations China should introduce what they call "social reform," by which they mean that it should turn to capitalism. . . . We must strive to clearly distinguish between people (many of them innocent young people) and the counter-revolutionaries and bad elements who have hoodwinked them, and whom we must deal with sternly and according to law.*[2]

Along with this speech, Deng and the government cracked down on many of the student protesters by arresting and imprisoning them. However, these actions did not quell the student protests.

Hu Yaobang, the Communist Party general secretary, encouraged many of the protesters. Hu agreed that it would be in the best interests of China to explore new ideas and create a new image. However, shortly after Hu expressed these views, more conservative members in the government challenged this idea, claiming it could only lead to dangerous Western ideas infiltrating the country. They feared this would cause social unrest and divert from the economic reforms already in place.

More Protests

By December 1986, student protests had erupted in 20 different cities around China. One hundred thousand students from 150 colleges and universities marched through the streets to demand freedom of speech, freedom of assembly and the press, and the opportunity to hold democratic elections. On January 1, 1987, a large student demonstration took place in Tiananmen Square. In the square, students burned copies of the newspapers that had most harshly criticized their efforts. Police quickly broke up the protest. Stern editorials in the daily Beijing newspaper followed, indicating that the government would not put up with more protests. Deng said these students had been poisoned by the ideas of troublemakers. Hu kept the student protesters from being sent to jail.

Conservative members of the Communist Party claimed that Hu had violated the principles of the party's leadership. In January 1987, after several weeks of student demonstrations, he was forced to resign as general secretary and Zhao Ziyang took his place. Meanwhile, the students, who had already been protesting against the government's response to the debate on social reform, launched new demonstrations.

The protests had ceased by mid-January, but China was still in crisis. Inflation increased, and farmers could not produce enough food to feed everyone. Workers who could not find jobs in rural areas moved to the cities. When they could not find work there, they were often

Leaflets

During the 1989 Tiananmen protests, students passed out leaflets to the soldiers sent to quell them. The leaflets warned the soldiers that the government was misleading them. They also assured them that the protesters did not harbor hatred but instead hoped there could be solidarity between them. Students also distributed leaflets to their fellow protesters with specific suggestions for how to handle confrontations with soldiers. Leaflets had been a common tool during earlier protests as well.

The students were not the only ones to attempt to change public opinion in this way. The Chinese government dropped leaflets by airplane over the square and the universities. The leaflets contained slogans for government supporters to use against the students, such as "Students, Return to Classes Immediately and Maintain Normal Educational Order!"[3] However, most citizens of Beijing shouted the students' slogans instead, such as "When Officials Oppress the People, the People Cannot Survive; When the Army Oppresses the People, the State Will Topple."[4]

forced to live on the streets. Some begged for food
or turned to crime as a means of survival. There was
corruption among government officials. Deng was
80 years old and ill. Many people believed he had
lost control of the government's Politburo, or ruling
committee. After ten years of Deng's reforms and
modernizations, China still struggled economically. ⁓

General Secretary Hu Yaobang supported the protesters.

Chapter 5

Students gathered to mourn Hu Yaobang on April 19, 1989.

THE PATRIOTIC DEMOCRATIC MOVEMENT

On April 15, 1989, Hu Yaobang, the fallen Communist Party leader, died suddenly of a heart attack. With his death, Hu become a hero to student activists, who felt he had suffered for their cause. Fang Lizhi, an astrophysicist and an advocate for human rights in China, talked about how Hu's death became a catalyst for action. He said,

> *Hu Yaobang himself wasn't that important, and the regard heaped on him was excessive. But in China, a leader's death serves as an excuse for people to assemble. The Party can't very well tell the people not to mourn a Party leader! Since a funeral is the only situation when people can assemble, you take advantage of the opportunity. It's only when people assemble that something can be achieved.*[1]

Students felt they had lost one of their few advocates. Hu's death not only provided a reason for students to gather but an opportunity to once again demonstrate for the freedoms of democracy.

As word of Hu's death spread, posters appeared on campuses with slogans such as "The Star of Hope Has Fallen" and "A Great Loss for Democracy and Freedom." On April 16, the first organized march of students mourning Hu took place. They marched to Tiananmen Square. A second march took place the next day—more than 4,000 people gathered in the square and chanted, "Long live freedom! Long live democracy! Down with corruption! Down with bureaucracy!"[2] China's police force, the Public Security Bureau (PSB), watched the protesters,

*Students in Tiananmen Square on the morning of
Hu Yaobang's memorial service*

but they were unarmed and made no effort to
interfere.

Another demonstration occurred the next day.
Several hundred students conducted a sit-in in
front of the Great Hall of the People in Tiananmen
Square. The students had a petition they hoped to
present to government officials, which proposed
items that included limits on corruption and the
privileges given to leaders, freedom of speech,
better funding for education, and the demand

that Hu's contributions to the country of China be more publicly appreciated. This time, there were members of the People's Armed Police (PAP)—who did carry weapons—in the square, but again they did not take action. In fact, behind the scenes, different government factions were debating how to best handle the situation.

Hu's memorial service took place in Tiananmen Square on April 22. The official service, which occurred inside the Great Hall of the People, was attended by 4,000 government officials. The funeral was much more ornate than a former party official would normally receive. The government hoped this would pacify the students and end the overwhelming discontent. Thousands of students had congregated in the square outside, and many of them had been there since the night before. Three student representatives carried the petition to the steps of the Great Hall. Kneeling respectfully, they asked to present the petition to Premier Li Peng, China's top leader since 1987, in person. When the premier did not respond, the students refused to give the petition to minor officials to pass on to Li. Angry at the lack of official response, they began boycotting their university classes.

PATRIOTIC DEMOCRATIC MOVEMENT

In the April 26, 1989, edition of the Beijing *People's Daily* newspaper, the government printed an editorial that accused a small number of people of stirring up unrest and attempting to overthrow the Communist Party. The editorial read,

> *An extremely small number of people with ulterior purposes continued to take advantage of the young students' feelings of grief for Comrade Hu Yaobang to spread all kinds of rumors to poison and confuse people's minds. . . . Blatantly violating the Constitution, they called for opposition to the leadership by the Communist Party and the socialist system.* [3]

This editorial sparked even larger demonstrations from the student protesters. On the following day, tens of thousands of students from all of Beijing's universities began to march toward Tiananmen Square, despite the fact that the editorial had warned of a possible violent crackdown on the protesters. Many of the students carried signs that showed their support for the Communist Party. They wanted to show they were not trying to overthrow the government or change to a Western-style democratic government as the editorial had suggested. They were just trying to change the corruption and privilege that had developed within the party and establish new freedoms.

As the students marched toward the square, citizens greeted them enthusiastically. As historian Frederic Wakeman explained, the signs carried by the students contained slogans that "guaranteed the support of a wide segment of the urban population suffering from rampant inflation, bribe-taking, and barely concealed economic exploitation."[4] The students represented the next leaders of China. The working people of Beijing sympathized with their cause; as

Premier Li Peng

When Li Peng was just three years old, his father, a writer who sympathized with the communists, was executed by the Nationalist Party. When Li was 11, he became the foster son of Zhou Enlai, a future premier and legendary figure of China. In 1948, Li was sent to the Soviet Union to study at the Moscow Power Institute, one of the leading technical universities in the country. Li's education as an engineer enabled him to return to China and work on several major power projects until 1979. He became a member of the Communist Party's Central Committee in 1982. Three years later, he became a member of the Politburo. In 1987, he became premier of China. Li kept this post until 1998.

Although Li was not the oldest person in the government, he joined a group known as the elders. The goal of this group was to slow down the pace of reform in China as well as limit the influence of Western culture. Li was responsible for declaring martial law in Beijing during the 1989 Tiananmen protests. Though condemned for his actions around the world, he insisted the incident was a historic victory for communism.

many as 500,000 people came out to watch the
students march.

As students and citizens flowed into Tiananmen
Square, the government sent representatives to
speak with them. But when these talks actually took
place a few days later, the students were not given
the opportunity to meet with any top leaders and
little was accomplished. As April drew to a close,
demonstrators still occupied the square. It was
obvious they needed to take further steps to make
their voices heard.

Protests during this time came to be known as
the Patriotic Democratic Movement, a name with
particular significance. The students hoped to bring
about a more democratic government, but they were
also proud of being Chinese. Most of the students
considered themselves patriots and did not explicitly
call for a Western type of government.

An Anniversary and a Visit

May 4, 1989, marked the seventieth anniversary
of the original 1919 protests in Tiananmen Square.
The students considered the occasion another
opportunity to voice their demands. As one Beijing
University student said,

We all knew from past experience that every one of the many student movements in modern China's history had ended in failure. Our only hope was that each new movement might help ever so slightly to change China's fate.[5]

Again, thousands of students, cheered on and followed by a large number of citizens, made their way to Tiananmen Square. The few sparse police lines were not enough to hold them back, but there was no open conflict or show of force. That same day, Zhao Ziyang, the general secretary of the Communist Party of China, suggested in a speech that the student protests were not a serious political problem. He recommended that the government consult with these students, since they were dedicated to improving the government, not overthrowing it. However, most other government officials felt threatened by the

Zhao Ziyang

Zhao Ziyang, the son of a wealthy landlord, was born in 1919 and joined the Young Communist League when he was 13. He helped introduce many agricultural reforms, which took farms out of a commune system and returned them to peasants in order to produce more food. He was successful with many other economic reforms as well. Zhao became premier in 1980 and stayed at that position until replacing Hu Yaobang as general secretary in 1987.

students. The way the government was organized did not provide the means to receive the opinions of Chinese citizens who were outside of official parties. Still, Zhao's unexpected support encouraged many students to give up their boycott of classes. They also felt they could not gain much more from continuing that tactic.

Another important event in May of that year was the planned visit to China by Soviet Union leader Mikhail Gorbachev. In his country, Gorbachev had managed to bring about economic reform as well as liberalize the Communist government. He represented the students' wishes for China. Gorbachev's visit was significant, marking the end of more than 20 years of strained relations between the two countries. Because of this, students saw the visit as an opportunity. They could put pressure on their government by interfering with the events.

The students had to decide how to continue to attract the support of regular citizens and make their voices heard. It was time to turn to a tactic that had long been a part of nonviolent social change around the world.

Students led a protest march through Tiananmen Square on May 4, 1989.

Students involved in the hunger strike rested on top of parked buses in Tiananmen Square.

RISING TENSIONS

On the weekend of May 13–14, 1989, the student protesters of the Patriotic Democratic Movement began using their new tactic—the hunger strike. In the same patriotic language utilized during the May Fourth Movement and the Cultural Revolution, the students announced their intentions in their "May 13 Hunger Strike Declaration":

> *In these bright and beautiful days of May, we are beginning a hunger strike. We are young, but we are ready to give up our lives. We cherish life: we do not want to die. But this nation is in a critical state. . . . At this life-and-death moment of the nation's fate, countrymen, please listen to us! China is our motherland. We are the people. The government should be our government. Who should speak out, if we should not? Who should act, if we should not?*[1]

The students who participated in the hunger strike seated themselves in the central area of Tiananmen Square and refused both food and drink. They became very weak and many fainted. Some students had to be hospitalized after just a few days of the hunger strike. This brought

Gorbachev's Visit

The visit to China by Soviet Union leader Mikhail Gorbachev drew a great deal of media attention. Gorbachev's visit was significant to the Chinese government because the Soviet Union had once dominated China and later became its rival. But on this visit, Gorbachev planned to acknowledge that the economic reform he was instituting was based on China's example. For this reason, China allowed a large number of foreign journalists and state-of-the-art communications technology into the country. This allowed the Tiananmen protests to be covered extensively by news stations around the world. Protests that occurred in other major Chinese cities were not as well documented around the globe.

more sympathy to the students from ordinary citizens.

The students were also drawing media attention, and they refused to clear the square for Gorbachev's visit. By the time the Soviet leader had arrived on May 15, approximately 3,000 students were participating in the hunger strike. Officials tried to keep the Soviet visitors away from the area.

Events scheduled to be held in or near the square were cancelled or relocated. Still, officials could not ignore the huge numbers of people at the square and the constant sound of ambulances for those who had collapsed.

With their Soviet visitors in the city, Chinese officials could

The Flying Tigers

As the army began making its way into Beijing, a group of young men with motorcycles, known as the Flying Tigers, carried out an important role. They rode from barricade to barricade, reporting on troop movements and sharing other information and news. Motorcycles were a luxury at this time, and these young men had previously been looked on with suspicion and envy. Reporter Shen Tong interviewed a Flying Tiger from his neighborhood:

"People like me have never had any status in this society, . . . We want the same things that you students are after. The officials are corrupt, but we're the ones who are looked down upon. This is the first time that the people of Beijing have recognized us," he said emotionally. "They actually respect us and like us. Everywhere I ride, the people yell, 'Long live the Flying Tigers!' It's worth dying for."[2]

do nothing about the protests, and the constant changes in plans were embarrassing and confusing. The student protesters felt their tactic had brought results. They also assumed, incorrectly, that the military would never be used against them and that the soldiers might join their side. The hunger strike did bring more support to the movement. One student commented, "The key was those seven days of hunger strike by several thousand students. It brought the people over to their side."[3]

MEETING WITH GOVERNMENT OFFICIALS

On May 18, Premier Li Peng visited a hospital and agreed to talk with some of the protesters. By that time, several students had stepped forward as leaders. Later that day, 22 student representatives came to the Great Hall of the People, some still exhausted and ill from their hunger strikes. One student leader, Wuer Kaixi, rushed to the hall from the hospital, where he had been recovering from his hunger strike. Wuer spoke with Li, but no progress was made. Both sides were confrontational. The students failed to show proper respect for the leaders. For his part, Li lectured the students, insisting that they end their hunger strike and warning that the government's patience was running out.

The next morning, Zhao made a surprise visit to the square. Zhao urged the students not to sacrifice themselves, warning,

> *Students, we came too late. We are sorry. . . . The reason that I came here is not to ask you to forgive us. All I want to say is that . . . you can't continue like this. . . . Now the situation is very serious . . . the Party and the nation is very antsy, the whole society is very worried. . . . if this situation continues, loses control, it will cause serious consequences at many places.*[4]

The students did not know that Zhao had lost the support of the Communist Party and would soon be stripped of his position as general secretary. Zhao had advocated for open discussion with the students. He had been the only one to disagree when the Politburo met and decided

Zhao Ziyang, center, spoke to the students during his surprise visit to Tiananmen Square.

to enforce martial law on Beijing. Once Gorbachev left the city, Zhao would no longer be able to protect the students.

Martial Law

After Zhao's visit to Tiananmen Square, even more people appeared on the streets to demonstrate

**Cui Jian:
China's Rock Star**

As the protests heated up, some of China's celebrities offered their support. Cui Jian is one of the most famous rock stars in the history of China. The students in Tiananmen Square chose one of his songs "Nothing to My Name" as their anthem. Cui performed at Tiananmen Square in mid-May. He sang "A Piece of Red Cloth," which was a song about isolation. He described that performance in an article for *Time* magazine: "I cover my eyes with a red cloth [while I was singing the song] to symbolize my feelings. The students were heroes. They needed me, and I needed them."[5]

against the government and ask officials to save the student protesters. Because so many of the hunger strikers were now dangerously ill, the students voted to cease the hunger strike but continue to occupy the square.

On May 19, Li called together party leaders and decided to declare martial law in parts of Beijing. This meant the army would be in control in those areas instead of the government law. The other party members backed Li, but Zhao was not present. He had lost his position in the party and was placed under house arrest, where he would remain for the rest of his life.

Li gave the protesters until 5:00 the next morning to vacate the square. After that, the army would move in. The students, however, refused to be intimidated. While some left, many thousands more remained. As one student recalled,

After the martial law decree, the number of people in the Square grew enormously. Everybody came into the Square, from every direction. This was an emergency. Everyone went.[6]

At dusk on Friday, May 19, soldiers from the People's Liberation Army (PLA) attempted to enter Beijing, even before martial law had been formally declared. The government wanted to take the protesters by surprise, but it was the army that was surprised. Every section of the incoming army was blocked—by local residents.

Craig Calhoun, a professor who was teaching in Beijing in the spring of 1989, described one scene as the PLA tried to enter the city:

Five open trucks and one bus of military police drove south in moderate traffic. Students with banners and flags moved into the path of these vehicles to stop them, halting other trucks and cars in front to make a roadblock. A substantial crowd of local people formed instantly. Drivers got out, and all joined in talking to the soldiers, telling them they had been brought to Beijing by a corrupt government and urging them not to attack the students. They agreed to turn back, to great applause from the crowd.[7]

Ordinary citizens crowded into the streets at all hours, even at night, to build barricades with trucks, buses, and garbage dumpsters. These citizens often pleaded with the army not to hurt the students. Most of the time, there was no clear organization to how citizens encountered the army. As one older woman put it, "We all had the same mind, the same idea. No one told us what to do. We just went out into the streets to stop the army."[8]

For the most part, the efforts of the people stopped the army from entering Beijing. Most soldiers retreated to the outskirts of the city. With this success, there was a new mood of defiance in Beijing. The success also inspired people in major cities all over China to demonstrate in solidarity. However, stopping the army also led to a stalemate—the students would not give in, and the silent government was unresponsive to the students' demands.

The Goddess Appears

By the end of May, morale among the students had fallen off. They needed a new source of inspiration to help them continue their cause. During the night of May 29, this new inspiration arrived in the form of a 33-foot-high (10 m) statue that would come to be known as the Goddess of Democracy. Students of the Central Academy of Fine Arts had built the statue. It looked somewhat similar to the Statue of Liberty, holding aloft a torch. Erected just across the square from a huge portrait of Mao, the statue became a rallying point and a symbol of the protest. The students hoped that even after they were gone, the statue would continue to stand as a reminder to the government that the square was the people's space.

As May drew to a close, tensions were high in Tiananmen Square, and conditions were deteriorating. With a lack of food and shelter and so much noise and activity, it was difficult for the protesters to sleep. As some students decided to end their occupation on May 30, other, more radical, groups vowed to continue until June 20. The PLA was

Building a Goddess

The students at the Central Academy of Fine Arts built the Goddess of Democracy statue to last as long as possible. Constructed from plastic foam, wire, and plaster, and made in four parts, the statue was easy to transport to the square. Once there, the pieces were assembled around a tall iron pole. Plaster was poured into the statue's hollow core, locking the pieces together. It was designed so that once the statue was put together, it could not be taken apart again. It would have to be destroyed all at once.

rumored to be preparing to move into the city again. Something would have to give, and it would happen soon. ⌒

Protesters put together the Goddess of Democracy.

*Protesters gave soldiers tea and attempted
to convince them to join the protest.*

THE CRACKDOWN

On the night of Friday, June 2, 1989, Tiananmen Square was crowded with students. Many were in poor health after a steady diet of just noodles and water. Yet despite these conditions, a new hunger strike was announced.

Rather than the large-scale hunger strike that had taken place in late May, this one would involve fewer people. However, many were high-profile figures, such as Chinese rock star Hou Dejian. Inspired by the actions of the students, he supported their cause. Hou's presence attracted even more students to Tiananmen Square. Many more ordinary civilians and workers had now joined the protests as well. It was no longer a simple student protest. Crowded together, everyone was nervously waiting to hear the sounds of approaching soldiers and military equipment.

The Army Moves In

Soldiers of the PLA had been visible around the city for several days. There were rumors that the soldiers were trying to ingratiate themselves with Beijing citizens, so they would be able to enter the city. Propaganda was broadcast on television to convince people to remain in their homes, warning that the army would use whatever force necessary to keep anyone from gathering in the streets. Most citizens remained firm in their determination to support and protect the protesters by stopping or impeding the army's progress.

Soldiers jumped barriers and entered Tiananmen Square.

Despite these actions, however, more than 10,000 soldiers made their way to the Great Hall of the People on Friday, June 2. Many were disguised in plainclothes to look like regular Beijing citizens. Other groups of soldiers attempting to enter the city were surrounded by citizens and prevented from moving. As additional soldiers moved into the area around Tiananmen Square, a group of cyclists traveled ahead of them, yelling to everyone that the army was on its way. Because no barricades had been put up along Changan Avenue, citizens who heard the news rushed outside to create any kind of barriers they could. However, because the soldiers were on foot, they simply scrambled over the barricades. Yet as the soldiers moved close to the square, they were met by a huge wall of people preventing them from entering.

JUNE 3

On the morning on June 3, more soldiers approached Tiananmen Square and took up their positions, although many were still hampered by citizens. Many skirmishes developed. People shouted and threw stones, and soldiers retaliated with firearms. Some protesters brutally beat soldiers and police officers. As the day wore on, people set fire to vehicles. Many citizens were injured or killed, shot by soldiers or crushed by tanks and other military vehicles. It was also falsely believed that soldiers would use rubber bullets to disperse the crowd. Many protesters had worn padded clothing or held up quilts to

Incident at Muxidi

One of the incidents that sparked violence between soldiers and citizens occurred on Friday night, June 3, when a military jeep ran over three cyclists and one pedestrian in an area west of Tiananmen called Muxidi. Three of the victims died. Citizens claimed the jeep had been going too fast. The government claimed the incident had been distorted as a way to provoke confrontations with the martial law troops. Many feel this incident set off Beijing's citizens, who were ready for a fight.

deflect such bullets, only to find that soldiers were using real ammunition. The troops had received orders to regain control of Tiananmen Square at all costs. They fired on anyone who tried to get in their way.

JUNE 4

As June 3 became the early hours of June 4, 1989, some of those in Tiananmen Square continued to carry out nonviolent protest and passive resistance. But chaos erupted as military vehicles and soldiers swept into the square. Some people rushed out of the square, while others stayed to protest. Following their orders to clear the square by morning, soldiers fired on some protesters.

A journalist for the Canadian Broadcasting Company (CBC), Tom Kennedy, described what he saw:

> I got to the northeast corner of the Square
> and could see soldiers firing, mostly into

"I ran into someone going in the opposite direction. He cried as he told me, 'They're killing people; many were killed around me.' Others began to cry with him as they heard the news. . . . I had to see for myself. . . . Flames lit the night sky as I got within a few hundred yards of [the intersection]. Soldiers, wielding machine guns, crouched behind armored personnel carriers. I couldn't believe that this was Beijing. . . . Then, at 12:30 a.m. on June 4, I saw the first corpse: a twenty-year-old man wearing a headband and a mask. He was lying on the concrete divider between the bicycle and automobile lanes."[1]

—A student from
Wuhan University

the south and southwest corner. An APC [armored personnel carrier] was in flames at the north end of the Square . . . the light from the flames reflected off their helmets. They walked slowly as they fired, and their rifles were on semi-automatic. They weren't firing into the ground or above people's heads —it was straight.[2]

At 4:00 a.m., all the lights in the square suddenly went out. When they came back on more than a half hour later, a tank had toppled the Goddess of Democracy statue. More soldiers had appeared and began to fire warning shots.

Approximately 3,000 protesters remained in the square. Around 4:30, one of the leaders of a labor union, whose members occupied the square, urged the other protesters to evacuate: "We must leave here immediately. . . . [T]he situation is now extraordinarily dangerous. To wish to die here is no more than an immature fantasy."[3] Other leaders urged the protesters to hold their ground—by shedding their blood and paying the price of their lives, they would secure democracy in China.

The four student leaders who had begun the hunger strike on June 2 tried to negotiate with the army to allow the protesters to leave safely. An hour later, several thousand protesters were allowed to leave the square at gunpoint.

The square was emptied, and police attempted to clear Changan Avenue and to cordon off Tiananmen Square to keep people from returning to it. More casualties took place in the streets around the square, as the soldiers were ordered to empty the streets as well. Ordinary citizens not involved in the protests often rushed to protect those in harm's way. But fully armed riot police shot at both protesters and citizens. More people, also expecting rubber bullets, were killed when they did not take cover. People joined hands and advanced toward the soldiers, singing, as guns fired around them.

Students and Others

Students were not the only ones protesting in Tiananmen Square in June 1989. Members of the new Beijing Workers Autonomous Federation (BWAF) also participated. They maintained their presence, despite an unwelcoming attitude by the students, who believed that workers did not have as much right to be there as educated students. The BWAF had been campaigning for workers' rights, and unlike the students, many of the members were prepared to fight to achieve their goals.

Many historians now believe that the Chinese government was more concerned about the BWAF than the students and cite the labor union as the ultimate reason for the crackdown. The Solidarity union in Poland had succeeded in overthrowing the Communist government there, and China was worried that a similar event could take place. Many believe the government's violent actions were a way of issuing a threat to the labor unions.

An eyewitness recalled,

> *You could see the guns firing, and people ran like crazy.
> Bullets ricocheted off the walls. . . . Some people went down.
> But after a while we all moved right back. It was like a dream.
> You were being shot at, and you can't believe you'd be so
> stupid as to go back again, but you do.*[4]

By 7:00 a.m. on June 4, Tiananmen Square
and its surrounding streets had been emptied of
people. No one knew exactly how many people had
been killed. Estimates ranged from hundreds to
even thousands of Chinese citizens and student
protesters. The Chinese government and its army
had crushed the movement and reasserted the
control of Beijing.

A City in Chaos

Beijing was in chaos. The streets were filled with
burning vehicles and broken glass, much of it from
the citizens' barricades. In the streets surrounding
the square, the dead and injured were everywhere.
The wounded were rushed to hospitals in any vehicle
that could be found. People wandered around
the city, dazed, looking for their friends. Citizens
still clashed angrily with soldiers and police, who

Counting the Dead

There is not an exact count of how many protesters and Beijing citizens died as a result of the Tiananmen Square events. The Chinese government did not want people to know how many casualties there were and concealed the number of dead. It is rumored that some bodies were taken away and burned before they could be counted. The government claims that 300 people were killed, but other estimates are as high as 6,000. The true count will never be known.

retaliated with gunfire. Within the square, other soldiers burned all traces of the student occupation, including tents and personal possessions, in huge bonfires. A cloud of thick black smoke obscured the Goddess of Democracy statue as it burned.

It would take days before Beijing returned to anything resembling normal. On June 5, the famous Tank Man made his stand on the city street and was made world famous by foreign news reporters' photographs of him. His image was just one of many that focused the eyes of the world on China and what had just occurred there. How would the world respond?

Some protesters ran for cover during the crackdown.

Tanks patrolled Beijing on June 6, 1989.

THE REACTION

After the events in Tiananmen Square, people in Beijing were in shock. Students slowly returned to their universities, telling their stories of the violence they had witnessed. They brought evidence with them: "The bulletin boards at the front of People's University by noon Sunday were covered with snapshots of the carnage, and bloody shirts and jackets were displayed on tree limbs by the main gate."[1] Other students arrived at their universities in trucks that carried the corpses of protesters.

OFFICIAL REACTIONS

On June 9, after rumors that he was ill or perhaps even dead, Deng appeared on Beijing television. He spoke of the incident as "a handful of bad people mixed with so many young students and onlookers."[2]

The government saturated the media with its own version of the events. It claimed that Tiananmen Square had been cleared peacefully; there had been no loss of life other than of "thugs" who tried to stop the army from doing its duty. Foreign journalists and students were expelled from the country. The government praised soldiers for their work in cleaning up the city. The leaders of the protests were also shown being arrested and led away. The government issued a most wanted list of 21 protest leaders. But by the time the list was issued, several of them were already escaping from China.

Soon people went back to work. Some students went back to classes. Everyone knew they were under constant surveillance from the government and were quiet and cautious. The government would later create documentaries using footage from cameras installed at street intersections. Much of the footage was edited to make it appear that the soldiers fired on citizens only after being attacked by them.

However, aided by the presence of foreign journalists who had been in China for Gorbachev's visit, images and news stories began flowing to every part of the world. Images, such as that of Tank Man, were instrumental in creating a public outcry against the Chinese government's actions.

Memorials

At some universities, professors and students organized events to commemorate what had happened at Tiananmen Square. At Jiaotong University in Shanghai, engineering students created a large metal wreath to be used in a commemoration ceremony. However, events such as these were quickly suppressed by the government, and the instigators were punished.

Most students and workers were afraid of the possibility of being arrested if they spoke out. For the next several anniversaries of the protests, people found ways to quietly mark the event. One popular method was for students to throw glass bottles out of their dorm room windows. In Chinese, *xiao ping* means "little bottle." Xiao ping is a homonym for Deng Xiaoping's name "Xiaoping." Using this technique, students could make a public commentary on the crackdown that was not likely to land them in trouble.

THE WORLD REACTS

Many of the foreign-relations gains made
by China in the five years of Deng's Four
Modernizations temporarily dissolved in the
aftermath of Tiananmen. The "open-door" policy
was suddenly closed again, as the exchange of
politicians between the United States and China
was suspended. President George H. W. Bush
announced a ban on any sales of military equipment
to China. The World Bank stopped lending China
money, and the International Monetary Fund
stopped work on all technical projects with China.
The European Union cancelled all high-level
contracts and loans and as of 2010 still maintained
an arms embargo against China. The Australian
government gave all Chinese students studying in
their country a four-year amnesty to remain there.

In addition to reactions that directly affected
China's economic and political relationships
with other countries, many world leaders released
statements that condemned the actions of the
Chinese government. The new humanitarian image
the Chinese government had tried to promote
throughout the 1980s suddenly seemed woefully
inaccurate.

Xi'an

One of the protests that occurred before the Tiananmen crackdown was in the city of Xi'an. On April 22, groups of students marched through the streets and were joined by unemployed workers. The demonstration quickly got out of control, and government party headquarters were set on fire. The firefighters who arrived to douse the flames also turned their hoses on the protesters, and a riot developed. Soon police were beating the demonstrators with sticks and clubs. Many people, including the elderly, women, and children, were injured. Witnesses saw the police dragging people behind police lines to beat them.

However, some world leaders expressed support for the actions taken by the Chinese government in the interests of maintaining their social stability. Singapore Senior Minister Lee Kuan Yew supported the government's decision to use force to control the protests. East Germany congratulated China for suppressing what it called "counterrevolutionary riots." And yet, to the people in many Communist Eastern Europe countries, the incident in Tiananmen Square was an inspiration to take action against their own governments. The protests at Tiananmen and the crackdown that followed are credited with sparking protests and ultimately the overthrow of Communist governments in some Eastern Europe countries, including East Germany, Czechoslovakia, Romania, Hungary, and by the end of 1991, even the Soviet Union.

Changan Avenue after the crackdown

RESTORING ORDER

Beijing remained under martial law until January 1990. In addition to the protest leaders being rounded up and sent to prison, others who had played a part in the demonstrations were relocated and forced to work in remote areas of China. Many students and teachers who had participated in the protests were politically marked and would never be employed again. Many were sent to the countryside. Even television news anchors who had sounded sympathetic to students during their coverage of the protests were fired.

Many of the more democratic changes being considered by reformers such as Zhao and others were quietly set aside. However, the protests did spark some changes in China.

Citizens in Hong Kong held a candlelight vigil on the twentieth anniversary of the Tiananmen Square crackdown.

*Guards at Tiananmen Square during the twentieth
anniversary of the protests*

THE LEGACY OF
TIANANMEN

While the situation did not change as much as protesters wished, the events at Tiananmen Square did have an effect on China. The government moved to change its relationship with the Chinese people by focusing exclusively on improving economic opportunity in the country. It created free markets for the growth of opportunity in business. This led to an explosion of China's economy in the 1990s. However, it also directly contributed to growing economic inequality and vastly different access to opportunity in different areas of China—particularly between cities and the countryside.

Moving Forward

The steps toward transforming China's economy have not been accompanied by many more political freedoms for its people. Depending on the type of criticism and the individual's position, some people who criticize the government of China are still given a long prison sentence. There are limited elections for government officials and not any for the highest-level leaders. Freedom of speech and of the press may be restricted depending on how threatening the content may seem to be. The government closely monitors the Internet, and certain Web sites are routinely censored or blocked entirely. While modest changes are occurring, the government continues to swiftly halt large-scale protests or organized calls for political reform.

An Anniversary

On June 4, 2009, the twentieth anniversary of the Tiananmen protests, Chinese and people around the world had many commemorations. In China, any commemoration had to be a private affair. Beijing was on lockdown. Many foreign news Web sites were blocked, dissidents were placed under house arrest, and police were present in large numbers in Tiananmen Square. Journalists were kept away from the scene. Any foreign magazines and newspapers with coverage of the anniversary were delivered with those pages torn out. Many of the Chinese people who lived through Tiananmen are still disturbed over what happened, and many young people seek to learn more about that time period.

In the following 20 years, China's economy became more and more closely linked to the global economy. In fact, China has become a major trading nation. In 2008, it had the second-largest economy in the world after the United States. However, like most large economies, its economic growth has not been without problems. The government does not closely regulate China's freewheeling market economy, and this has led to significant problems with environmental degradation, worker abuse, trade in illegal products, and tainted consumer goods. It is common in the Chinese media to see reports of products found to be harmful to consumers. Some of these—including toys with lead paint—have even been exported to the United States.

As of 2010, most people in China still avoided talking about what happened at Tiananmen Square in 1989. This is partly due to the government's actions in suppressing information about the protests and partly to the threat of retaliation for speaking out against the government. Perhaps the largest influence is that the younger, post-Tiananmen generation knows very little about the protests of 1989, and they see their future more closely tied to opportunities in the economy than in politics. People in China still stage protests—some with protesters numbering in the thousands. These protests, however, focus on issues such as unemployment or environmental degradation.

What If?

If the Tiananmen Square protests had succeeded, and the government had not used violence to dispel the protesters, what might have happened? The protest movement might have swept across the entire country to include not only students. Even more members of labor unions and regular citizens may have joined in. Perhaps China's communist government would have fallen, just as many Eastern European Communist countries did.

However, Chinese leaders feared that the introduction of more freedom of speech and free

The modern city of Beijing

elections would have resulted in chaos. The
government claims that it would not have been
possible to modernize China and its economy in
this case. In an interview with CNN, Zhu Muzhi,
secretary-general of the China Society for Human
Rights Studies, said,

> *[T]he way that the June 4 turmoil was dealt with was*
> *completely correct. If it had not been dealt with in that way*
> *at that point, I think that China's situation would not be*
> *the same today. . . . Everyone would have been fighting,*
> *fighting the common people, fighting amongst the masses.*

Domestically China couldn't have quickly returned to peace and stability, and it would have been impossible for the economy to continue its fast pace of development. . . . I think that time has shown that things at that time were handled correctly.[1]

Other Chinese citizens, after seeing how Russia has fared since the collapse of the Soviet Union, feel that the crackdown was necessary to maintain order and bring the economic advances that China has enjoyed since 1989. Russia has moved toward a democratic government, but many of its people suffer from extreme poverty and a lack of stability as a result. Without the forced disbanding of the protesters, the Chinese people might not be witnessing the economic prosperity they have today.

MISTAKES AT TIANANMEN

Twenty years after the Tiananmen Square protests, many historians feel the student movement was self-defeating and could never have succeeded using the tactics that it did. Liu Binyan, an exiled Chinese journalist, stated,

One of the important reasons for the Tiananmen Movement's failure is that at the peak of the movement, both the students

and the government had some illusions. The government felt for the first time ever as if it were on the verge of being toppled; the student leaders thought once the government sent troops to the Square, the whole nation would rise up to their call, thus leading to the collapse of the government. But neither of these two illusions were true.[2]

Liu also feels that the students ignored the workers and peasants of China, who could have joined them in their protests. And, because many of the students were from wealthy families, they had contempt

Insider Accounts

Several insider accounts and documents about the Tiananmen Square protests have been smuggled out of China and published. In 2001, Zhang Liang, who became a member of the Chinese government after the protests, left China for the United States. There, he published a book of official government documents from the events. *The Tiananmen Papers* revealed information, such as details about what took place in the government and the related power struggles. However, some have questioned the book's authenticity, citing the use of expressions that are not used in Chinese dialect. They also identify sections that may have been plagiarized or fabricated.

After the Tiananmen Square protests, Zhao Ziyang was stripped of his title and spent the next 16 years of his life under house arrest. During this time, Zhao secretly recorded tapes of his experiences around the time of the protests. After Zhao's death in 2005, the tapes were found and smuggled out of the country. In 2009, these tapes were formed into a book, *Prisoner of the State*. The book reveals Zhao's attempts to avoid imposing martial law during the Tiananmen Square protests. It is also made clear that Zhao had already been butting heads with other government officials prior to the events of 1989.

for these other members of Chinese society. Not only did they not try to win them over to their cause, they refused to allow them to participate. The students also refused any kind of compromise that might have prevented the bloodshed at Tiananmen.

The Legacy

While the events at Tiananmen Square did not change China's political system, there is a lasting legacy. Some former leaders of the protests who were exiled from China, such as Han Dongfang and Wang Dan, still hope to bring about change. Meanwhile, new protests have taken place. Laborers have gone on strike to bring attention to rising prices, industrial safety, working conditions, and unpaid wages. Often, the workers' demands are met to avoid further unrest, although the government often deals with the leaders of these strikes harshly.

Many ordinary Chinese citizens who experienced the events of 1989 feel that the protesters were justified. While they may not speak out for fear of government reprisal, they remember the dreams of that time and the possibilities for a different direction to China's reform. Still others see the tremendous economic progress that China has made since that time and admit that China has developed beyond the wildest dreams of those protesters. Many people now believe political change can be accomplished only by working within the existing Chinese government. But there is always the possibility that the quest for change may lead protesters to Tiananmen Square once again.

Tiananmen Square

TIMELINE

1919

On May 4, students stage a protest in Tiananmen Square against the Treaty of Versailles.

1949

Mao Zedong proclaims the establishment of the People's Republic of China.

1981

Hu Yaobang is appointed as general secretary of the Communist Party in June.

1986

In late fall, students stage a series of protests to demand political reform.

1987

Hu Yaobang is forced to resign. Zhao Ziyang becomes general secretary and Li Peng becomes premier.

1966–1976

The Cultural Revolution occurs. Universities close and then reopen only to those from preferred social classes.

1978

Deng Xiaoping launches the Four Modernizations. A stretch of wall in Beijing becomes known as the Democracy Wall.

1989

Hu Yaobang dies of a heart attack on April 15, and people begin to gather in Tiananmen Square.

1989

Three students attempt to present a petition to Premier Li Peng on April 22. Students begin boycotting university classes.

1989

On April 26, the *People's Daily* newspaper publishes an editorial accusing a "handful of plotters" of stirring unrest.

TIMELINE

1989

1989

1989

On April 27, students from more than 40 universities march to Tiananmen Square to protest the editorial.

On May 13, hundreds of students begin a hunger strike in the square.

On May 15, Soviet leader Mikhail Gorbachev arrives in Beijing, bringing international media attention to the city.

1989

1989

1989

On June 3 at 10:00 p.m., soldiers clear the square and surrounding streets. Many people are killed.

On June 4, by 1:00 a.m., soldiers completely surround Tiananmen Square.

On June 4 around 4:00 a.m., negotiations take place to allow students to leave the square.

1989

On May 18, Li Peng summons student leaders to the Great Hall of the People for a talk, but nothing is achieved.

1989

The government formally declares martial law on May 20, but students and citizens block the army's advance into Beijing.

1989

On the night of May 29, the Goddess of Democracy statue arrives in the square.

1989

On June 4 around 5:00 a.m., students depart the square at gunpoint.

1989

On June 5, Tank Man confronts the army tanks near Tiananmen Square. His image becomes a symbol of the events there.

2009

On June 4, the twentieth anniversary of the protests are observed around the world but forbidden in public in China.

ESSENTIAL FACTS

DATE OF EVENT

April 1989–June 4, 1989

PLACE OF EVENT

Tiananmen Square, Beijing, China

KEY PLAYERS

- Deng Xiaoping
- Hu Yaobang
- Li Peng
- Zhao Ziyang
- Thousands of protesters—students, workers, and citizens of Beijing

HIGHLIGHTS OF EVENT

❖ Beginning in mid-April 1989, Chinese university students gathered in Tiananmen Square to demand a more democratic government. Using nonviolent principles, they staged a sit-in and hunger strikes and attempted to talk with government officials to voice their concerns.

❖ Communist Party leaders refused to meet with them, and the number of students in the square increased.

❖ The government threatened to declare martial law and use the army to clear the square. When martial law was announced, Beijing citizens erected barricades and kept the army from advancing into the city.

❖ On June 3, the army finally made its way into the city and used violence to retake control of Tiananmen Square, killing hundreds or perhaps even thousands of students, teachers, citizens, and bystanders. The square was cleared by June 4.

❖ A young man who became known outside China as Tank Man stood in front of advancing army tanks, refusing to move. His image became a symbol of the Tiananmen events.

❖ A few months after the protest, the government passed a law restricting public gatherings and rallies.

❖ In China today, most young people do not know much about the events that occurred in Tiananmen Square, and images of the period are blocked on the Internet and in the media.

QUOTE

"I pledge to use my young life to defend Tiananmen and to defend the republic. My head may be cut off, the blood may flow, but Tiananmen Square must not be lost. I will fight until the last person falls."—*oath sworn by some students occupying Tiananmen Square on June 3, 1989*

ADDITIONAL RESOURCES

SELECT BIBLIOGRAPHY

Brook, Timothy. *Quelling the People: The Military Suppression of the Beijing Democracy Movement*. New York: Oxford University Press, 1992.

Calhoun, Craig. *Neither Gods nor Emperors: Students and the Struggle for Democracy in China*. Berkeley, CA: University of California Press, 1994.

Feigon, Lee. *The Meaning of Tiananmen: China Rising*. Chicago, IL: Ivan R. Dee, 1990.

Zhao, Dingxin. *The Power of Tiananmen: State–Society Relations and the 1989 Beijing Student Movement*. Chicago, IL: University of Chicago Press, 2001.

FURTHER READING

Barth, Kelly, ed. *At Issue in History: The Tiananmen Square Massacre*. San Diego, CA: Greenhaven Press, 2003.

Bingham, Jane. *Days That Shook the World: Tiananmen Square June 4, 1989*. Chicago, IL: Raintree, 2004.

Sebag-Montefiore, Poppy. *Eyewitness China*. New York: Dorling Kindersley, 2007.

Web Links

To learn more about the Tiananmen Square protests, visit ABDO Publishing Company online at **www.abdopublishing.com**. Web sites about the Tiananmen Square protests are featured on our Book Links page. These links are routinely monitored and updated to provide the most current information available.

Places to Visit

International Civil Rights Center and Museum
134 South Elm Street, Greensboro, NC 27401
336-274-9199
www.sitinmovement.org/home.html
This museum is dedicated to the struggle for human rights and the use of nonviolent protest.

Museum of Chinese in America
215 Centre Street, New York, NY 10013
212-619-4785
www.mocanyc.org
This museum houses exhibits on the experiences and history of Chinese Americans.

GLOSSARY

capitalism
An economic system in which the resources used to produce goods are privately owned. A capitalist country is governed by the principles of a free market economy: supply and demand.

communism
A political system in which the resources used to produce goods are commonly owned by all members of a society. In practice in China and the Soviet Union, however, the state as the representative of the people owned these resources.

counterrevolution
A revolution to overthrow the current government system, which itself was established by a revolution.

democracy
A government in which citizens exercise power by voting and electing leaders to represent them.

exploitation
The use or abuse of someone or something for selfish gains.

general secretary
The head of the Communist Party in China.

house arrest
Confinement of an arrested person in his or her residence instead of jail.

hunger strike
> The deliberate refusal to eat as a form of protest.

liberalization
> The process of becoming more accepting of new ideas and changes.

martial law
> Temporary control of a country by the army.

Politburo
> The executive committee of the ruling Communist Party.

premier
> Head of a government.

socialism
> A social system based on collective achievement and sharing of wealth.

suppress
> To prohibit or limit the activities of a person or a group, or to keep something from being revealed.

Western
> Referring to the United States and Europe.

Source Notes

Chapter 1. Taking a Stand

1. Craig Calhoun. *Neither Gods Nor Emperors: Students and the Struggle for Democracy in China*. Berkeley, CA: University of California Press, 1997. 131.

2. Ibid. 133.

3. Patrick Witty. "Behind the Scenes: Tank Man of Tiananmen." *New York Times Lens Blog*. 3 June 2009. 23 Oct. 2009 <http://lens.blogs.nytimes.com/2009/06/03/behind-the-scenes-tank-man-of-tiananmen/?scp=1&sq=behind%20the%20scenes%20tank%20man%20of%20tiananmen&st=cse>.

4. James Barron. "Crackdown in Beijing: One Man Can make a Difference: This One Jousted Briefly with Goliath." *New York Times*. 6 June 1989. 23 Oct. 2009 <http://www.nytimes.com/1989/06/06/world/crackdown-beijing-one-man-can-make-difference-this-one-jousted-briefly-with.html>.

Chapter 2. A History of Protests

1. Lee Feigon. *China Rising: The Meaning of Tiananmen*. Chicago, IL: Ivan R. Dee, 1990. 27.

Chapter 3. Setting the Stage

1. Craig Calhoun. *Neither Gods Nor Emperors: Students and the Struggle for Democracy in China*. Berkeley, CA: University of California Press, 1997. 9.

Chapter 4. Students Speaking Out
1. Wei Jingsheng. "Unorthodox Opinions Are Heard on the Street." *Time Asia*. 27 Sept. 1999. 23 Oct. 2009 <http://www.time.com/time/asia/magazine/99/0927/democracy_wall.html>.
2. Deng Xiaoping. "Uphold the Four Cardinal Principles." 30 Mar. 1979. 23 Oct. 2009 <http://english.people.com.cn/dengxp/vol2/text/b1290.html>.
3. Timothy Brook. *Quelling the People: The Military Suppression of the Beijing Democracy*. New York: Oxford University Press, 1992. 61.
4. Ibid. 62.

Chapter 5. The Patriotic Democratic Movement
1. Timothy Brook. *Quelling the People: The Military Suppression of the Beijing Democracy*. New York: Oxford University Press, 1992. 21.
2. Ibid. 22.
3. "It Is Necessary to Take a Clear-Cut Stand Against Disturbances." *Beijing People's Daily*. 26 Apr. 1989. 23 Oct. 2009 <http://www.tSquare.tv/chronology/April26ed.html>.
4. Timothy Brook. *Quelling the People: The Military Suppression of the Beijing Democracy*. New York: Oxford University Press, 1992. 33.
5. Ibid. 34.

SOURCE NOTES CONTINUED

Chapter 6. Rising Tensions
1. "The May 13 Hunger Strike Declaration (1989)." *Columbia University Asia for Educators*. 23 Oct. 2009 <http://afe.easia.columbia.edu/ps/china/tiananmen_hunger_strike.pdf>.
2. Craig Calhoun. *Neither Gods Nor Emperors: Students and the Struggle for Democracy in China*. Berkeley, CA: University of California Press, 1997. 95.
3. Timothy Brook. *Quelling the People: The Military Suppression of the Beijing Democracy*. New York: Oxford University Press, 1992. 39.
4. "Tiananmen Square, June Fourth Movement, 1989." Facsimile. June 2007. 23 Oct. 2009 < http://www.facsimilemagazine.com/2007/06/index.html>.
5. Cui Jian. "The Idol: The Spirit Lives In Rock 'n' Roll." *Time*. 4 Oct. 1999. 12 May 2010 <http://www.time.com/time/magazine/article/0,9171,992171,00.html>.
6. Timothy Brook. *Quelling the People: The Military Suppression of the Beijing Democracy*. New York: Oxford University Press, 1992. 44.
7. Craig Calhoun. *Neither Gods Nor Emperors: Students and the Struggle for Democracy in China*. Berkeley, CA: University of California Press, 1997. 89.
8. Jane Bingham. *Days That Shook the World: Tiananmen Square June 4, 1989*. Chicago, IL: Raintree, 2004. 25.

Chapter 7. The Crackdown

1. Craig Calhoun. *Neither Gods Nor Emperors: Students and the Struggle for Democracy in China*. Berkeley, CA: University of California Press, 1997. 129.
2. Timothy Brook. *Quelling the People: The Military Suppression of the Beijing Democracy*. New York: Oxford University Press, 1992. 136.
3. Craig Calhoun. *Neither Gods Nor Emperors: Students and the Struggle for Democracy in China*. Berkeley, CA: University of California Press, 1997. 135.
4. Ibid. 138.

Chapter 8. The Reaction

1. Timothy Brook. *Quelling the People: The Military Suppression of the Beijing Democracy*. New York: Oxford University Press, 1992. 154.
2. Deng Xiaoping. "June 9 Speech to Martial Law Units." Beijing Domestic Television Service. 9 June 1989. 23 Oct. 2009 <http://www.tSquare.tv/chronology/Deng.html>.

Chapter 9. The Legacy of Tiananmen

1. Rebecca MacKinnon. "Chinese human rights official says the crackdown 'completely correct'." *CNN.com*. 2 June 1999. 23 Oct. 2009 <http://www.cnn.com/WORLD/asiapcf/9906/02/tiananmen/MacKinnon/zhu.muzhi.html>.
2. Kelly Barth. *At Issue in History: The Tiananmen Square Massacre*. San Diego, CA: Greenhaven Press, 2003. 91.

INDEX

ABOUT THE AUTHOR

Marcia Amidon Lusted is the author of more than 30 books
for young readers. She is an assistant editor for Cobblestone
Publishing, a writing instructor, and a musician. Lusted lives in
New Hampshire with her family.

PHOTO CREDITS

Jeff Widener/AP Images, cover, 3, 15, 67; Reuters/CORBIS, 6,
99 (bottom); Peter Turnley/CORBIS, 9, 98; North Wind Picture
Archive, 16; AP Images, 23, 27, 28, 31, 96, 97 (top); Jacques
Langevin/Corbis, 37; Bettmann/CORBIS, 38; Pascal George/
AFP/Getty Images, 45; Catherine Henriette/AFP/Getty Images,
46, 56, 97 (bottom); Sadayuki Mikami/AP Images, 48, 55, 99
(top); Xinhua/AP Images, 61; Patrick Durand/Corbis, 68; Thomas
Cheng/AFP/Getty Images, 70; Durand-Langevin/Sygma/Corbis,
77; Vincent Yu/AP Images, 78; David Turnley/CORBIS, 83; Paul
Hilton/Corbis, 85; Elizabeth Dalziel/AP Images, 86; Yong Hian
Lim/iStockphoto, 90; Steve Geer/iStockphoto, 95